Over 50 Variations on the Campfire Classic

So S'MORE to Do

by Becky Rasmussen

Adventure Publications, Inc.
Cambridge, Minnesota

Cover design by Jonathan Norberg

Book design by Lora Westberg

Edited by Ryan Jacobson

Illustrations by Erik Ahlman

10 9 8 7 6 5 4 3 2

Copyright 2010 by Becky Rasmussen
Published by Adventure Publications, Inc.
820 Cleveland Street South
Cambridge, MN 55008
1-800-678-7006
www.adventurepublications.net

ISBN: 978-1-59193-267-3

This book is dedicated to Jen and Ann, whose encouragement could inspire me no s'more!

Table of Contents

GOURMET S'MORES

GRAHAM ALTERNATIVES

NUTTY ABOUT S'MORES

S'MORE FOR THE HOLIDAYS

S'MORES FOR ADULTS

Introduction

For many years, s'mores have been an essential part of the camping experience. While the original is always a tasty standby, most people have never thought to challenge the limits of the s'more.

This book is broken into seven different sections to help you expand your s'more imagination. There are also spaces provided in the back of this book for you to invent your own s'more concoctions. I invite you to test your limits, open your mind, and try some of my favorite recipes. Let your creative juices flow—and enjoy!

Did You Know?

The name of this tasty campfire treat comes from combining the words "some more," because once you have one, you'll be begging for seconds!

History of the S'more

Marshmallow candy originated in ancient Egypt some 4,000 years ago, but s'mores are relatively new to the world. The good news is that *someone* invented s'mores in the early 1900s (not long after marshmallows became mass-produced and nationally distributed). The bad news is that no one knows exactly who, when or where s'mores were created, so we cannot thank a specific person for this delectable dessert.

We can guess that the original recipe was devised around a campfire, putting to use ingredients—marshmallows, graham crackers and chocolate—that were easy to pack and carry. Through the years that followed, the recipe was passed from person to person until it found its way into the *Girl Scout Handbook* in 1927.

The rest, as they say, is history.

Marshmallow Toasting Guide

Everyone has their own interpretation of how a perfectly toasted marshmallow looks and tastes. For reference, I have provided the following guide to help you identify your personal toasting preference:

Perfection Only

Lightly browned on all sides of the marshmallow. If your marshmallow burns or catches fire, waste no time in starting over with a fresh one.

How to: Using your metal skewer (a stick just will not do) place a lone marshmallow beside the flames and above the embers. Rotate your marshmallow, and don't stop rotating until its center begins to sag off the skewer. Eat quickly; this little piece of perfection won't stay perfect for long.

Slightly Past Perfection

Browned on most sides with a few scorch marks. The marshmallow is thoroughly warmed with a little extra flavor.

How to: Your technique is similar to the perfectionist's, except you have more room for "error." Use a stick. Cook multiple marshmallows together. Toast one side at a time. It doesn't matter; it's all good!

En Flambe

A flaming marshmallow is a good marshmallow. It will be thoroughly blackened and crunchy on the outside with the possibility of still being cold on the inside.

How to: Stick your marshmallow into the fire. Let it burn for a moment. Extinguish. Eat. Could it be any simpler?

Warmed by Technology

If cooking over an open flame isn't your idea of a good time, the microwave can easily be the next best thing. After all, who needs the bugs? (The microwave is also a great solution for snowy months and rainy days.)

How to: Put your marshmallow on a plate, and cook it for 10 to 20 seconds. The marshmallow will expand while it heats up, but it will shrink again as it cools. When the marshmallow is almost back to normal size, it's ready to eat.

Note: Recipes provided in this cookbook are compatible with all marshmallow toasting styles.

How to Build the Perfect Campfire

There are two key elements to creating the perfect campfire for roasting marshmallows: planning and patience. When using them both, anyone can do it.

Planning

To build a campfire, start by placing one log in the fire pit. Turn 4–5 additional logs on end and lean them together building a pyramid- or tepee-like tower over the first log. Fill the space beneath the tower with kindling: newspaper, twine, small sticks and twigs. Light the kindling (newspaper), and soon you should have a roaring blaze. Allow your campfire to burn down for at least 10–15 minutes before you start roasting marshmallows.

Patience

Sometimes it takes a while, but waiting for your logs to burn down will give you a warmer fire with better coals for toasting. There will also be smaller, more predictable flames, so your marshmallow will be less likely to burn.

The Original S'more

Ingredients

Marshmallows
Graham Crackers
Chocolate Bars

Building Instructions

Toast marshmallow to the desired level. Sandwich the
marshmallow and desired amount of chocolate between
two graham cracker halves.

Chocolate Bar Substitutes

Your new favorite campfire concoction might be as simple as swapping out the chocolate bar!

Ingredients

Marshmallows
Graham Crackers
~~Chocolate Bars~~

Building Instructions

Toast marshmallow to the desired level. Place desired amount of candy bar and the marshmallow on half of a graham cracker. Top the marshmallow with another half of a graham cracker.

1. Chocolate peanut butter cups
2. White chocolate bars
3. Dark chocolate bars
4. Chocolate crunch bars
5. Your favorite candy bar

BROWNIE S'MORES

Ingredients

  Marshmallows
  Graham Crackers
  Brownies

Prep Work

Using your favorite brownie mix, prepare as directed on the package. Use the largest pan size to make thin brownies. Bake and cool. Cut the brownies into 2" x 2" squares.

Building Instructions

Toast marshmallow to the desired level. Place a brownie and the toasted marshmallow on half of a graham cracker. Top the marshmallow with another half of a graham cracker.

Crunchy Granola S'mores

Ingredients

- Marshmallows
- Graham Crackers
- Sweetened Granola

Building Instructions

Toast marshmallow to the desired level. Place granola on half of a graham cracker. Sandwich the marshmallow and granola bits together with another half of a graham cracker.

Chocolate Fudge
Sundae S'mores

Ingredients

Marshmallows
Graham Crackers
Chocolate Fudge Frosting
Chocolate Sundae Syrup

Building Instructions

Frost half of a graham cracker with chocolate fudge frosting.
Toast marshmallow to the desired level. Place marshmallow
on the frosted graham cracker, and top with sundae syrup.
Sandwich the marshmallow and chocolate together with
another half of a graham cracker.

Tropical S'mores

Ingredients

Marshmallows
Graham Crackers
Mixed Dried Fruit Pieces
   (Pineapple, Apricot, Mango)
Marshmallow Creme

Building Instructions

Frost half of a graham cracker
with marshmallow creme. Toast
marshmallow to the desired level.
Place desired amount of fruit on the frosted graham cracker.
Sandwich the marshmallow and fruit pieces together with
another half of a graham cracker.

Sprinkle S'mores

Ingredients

    Marshmallows
    Graham Crackers
    Sprinkles
    Whipped Cream

Building Instructions

Frost half of a graham cracker with whipped cream. Shake desired amount of sprinkles onto the frosted graham cracker. Toast marshmallow to the desired level. Place marshmallow on the frosted graham cracker. Sandwich the marshmallow and sprinkles together with another half of a graham cracker.

CINNAMON TOAST S'MORES

Ingredients

Marshmallows
Cinnamon Graham Crackers

Building Instructions

Toast marshmallow to the desired
level. Place toasted marshmallow
on half of a graham cracker.
Sandwich the marshmallow
with another half of a
graham cracker.

Peanut Butter & Banana S'mores

Ingredients

Marshmallows
Graham Crackers
Peanut Butter
Bananas

Building Instructions

Peel bananas and cut into slices. Spread peanut butter on half of a graham cracker. On top of the peanut butter, place banana slices. Toast marshmallow to the desired level. Place marshmallow on top of the banana slices. Sandwich the marshmallow and banana slices together with another half of a graham cracker.

Marshmallow–
A-Holic S'mores

Ingredients

Marshmallows
Graham Crackers
Marshmallow Creme

Building Instructions

Frost half of a graham cracker with marshmallow creme.
Toast marshmallow to the desired level. Place marshmallow
on the frosted graham cracker. Sandwich the marshmallow
and marshmallow creme together with another half of a
graham cracker.

Apple Cinnamon Raisin S'mores

Ingredients

Marshmallows
Cinnamon Graham Crackers
Apples
Raisins

Building Instructions

Cut apples into slices. Place apple slices on half of a cinnamon graham cracker. Place raisins on top of apple slices. Toast marshmallow to the desired level. Place toasted marshmallow on top of the apples and raisins. Sandwich the marshmallow with another half of a cinnamon graham cracker.

Peanut Butter & Jelly S'mores

Ingredients

Marshmallows
Graham Crackers
Peanut Butter
Jelly (any flavor)

Building Instructions

Spread peanut butter on half
of a graham cracker. Spread
jelly on another half of a graham
cracker. Toast marshmallow to
the desired level. Place marshmallow on the
peanut-butter-covered graham cracker. Sandwich
together with the jelly-covered graham cracker.

STRAWBERRY SHORTCAKE S'MORES

Ingredients

Marshmallows
Graham Crackers
Strawberry Pie Filling
Vanilla Frosting

Building Instructions

Frost half of a graham cracker with vanilla frosting. Place one scoop of strawberry pie filling on the frosted graham cracker. Toast marshmallow to the desired level. Place marshmallow on top of the strawberry pie filling. Sandwich the marshmallow and pie filling together with another half of a graham cracker.

Chocolate-Covered Potato Chip S'mores

Ingredients

Marshmallows
Graham Crackers
Rippled Potato Chips
Chocolate Chips
Butter

Prep Work

Melt a bag of semi-sweet chocolate chips with 2 tablespoons of butter. Stir chocolate until smooth. Dunk potato chips into the chocolate mixture until only a small portion of the potato chips are uncovered. Use a spoon to remove excess chocolate. Place potato chips on a sheet of wax paper, and refrigerate until the chocolate has hardened.

Building Instructions

Toast marshmallow to the desired level. Place the toasted marshmallow on half of a graham cracker. Sandwich marshmallow and a chocolate-covered potato chip together with another half of a graham cracker.

Cookies & Cream S'mores

Ingredients

Marshmallows
Graham Crackers
Oreo® Cookies
Marshmallow Creme

Prep Work

In a large, resealable plastic bag, crush cookies into large
pieces with a rolling pin.

Building Instructions

Frost half of a graham cracker with marshmallow creme.
Sprinkle cookie pieces onto the frosted graham cracker.
Toast marshmallow to the desired level. Place marshmallow
on top of cookie pieces. Sandwich the marshmallow and
cookie pieces together with another half of a graham cracker.

Butter Brickle S'mores

Ingredients

- Marshmallows
- Graham Crackers
- Chocolate-Covered Toffee Bars
- Vanilla Frosting

Prep Work

In a large, resealable plastic bag, crush toffee bars into large pieces with a rolling pin.

Building Instructions

Frost half of a graham cracker with vanilla frosting. Sprinkle toffee bar pieces onto the frosted graham cracker. Toast marshmallow to the desired level. Place marshmallow on top of toffee bar pieces. Sandwich the marshmallow and toffee bar pieces together with another half of a graham cracker.

Tiramisu S'mores

Ingredients

Marshmallows
Graham Crackers
Vanilla Frosting
Nilla® Wafers
Cocoa

Building Instructions

Frost two graham cracker halves
with vanilla frosting. Sprinkle cocoa
onto one of the graham cracker halves.
On the other frosted graham cracker,
place wafers. Toast marshmallow to the desired level. Place
marshmallow on top of the wafers. Sandwich the marshmallow and wafers together with the other graham cracker.

PISTACHIO S'MORES

Ingredients

Marshmallows
Graham Crackers
Chocolate Bars
Pistachio Pudding

Prep Work

Using a pistachio pudding mix, prepare as directed on the package, but use only ¾ cup of milk. This will make the pudding thicker and easier to spread. Chill.

Building Instructions

Frost half of a graham cracker with pistachio pudding. Place chocolate bar pieces on the frosted graham cracker. Toast marshmallow to the desired level. Place marshmallow on top of chocolate bar pieces. Sandwich the marshmallow and chocolate bar pieces together with another half of a graham cracker.

Chocolate-Covered Strawberry S'mores

Ingredients

Marshmallows
Graham Crackers
Strawberries
Chocolate Chips
Butter
Chocolate Sundae Syrup

Prep Work

Clean strawberries and remove stems. Slice strawberries into pieces. Melt a bag of semi-sweet chocolate chips with 2 tablespoons of butter. Stir until smooth. Dunk strawberry pieces into the chocolate mixture. Use a spoon to remove excess chocolate. Place strawberry pieces on a sheet of wax paper, and refrigerate until the chocolate has hardened.

Building Instructions

On half of a graham cracker, place chocolate-covered strawberry pieces. Toast marshmallow to the desired level. Place the marshmallow on top of the strawberry pieces. Drizzle chocolate sundae syrup over the marshmallow. Sandwich together with another half of a graham cracker.

After Dinner Mint S'mores

Ingredients

- Marshmallows
- Graham Crackers
- Chocolate Frosting
- Andes® Mints

Building Instructions

Frost half of a graham cracker with chocolate frosting. Place mints on the frosted graham cracker. Toast marshmallow to the desired level. Place marshmallow on top of the mints. Sandwich the marshmallow and mints together with another half of a graham cracker.

Caramel Apple S'mores

Ingredients

Marshmallows
Graham Crackers
Apples
Caramel Sundae Syrup

Building Instructions

Cut apples into slices. Place apple slices on half of a graham cracker. Drizzle caramel sundae syrup over apples. Toast marshmallow to the desired level. Place marshmallow on top of the apples. Sandwich the marshmallow and apples together with another half of a graham cracker.

Coconut S'mores

Ingredients

- Marshmallows
- Graham Crackers
- Coconut Flakes
- Vanilla Frosting

Building Instructions

Frost half of a graham cracker with vanilla frosting. Sprinkle coconut flakes onto the frosted graham cracker. Toast marshmallow to the desired level. Place marshmallow on top of the coconut flakes. Sandwich the marshmallow and coconut together with another half of a graham cracker.

BANANA CREAM PIE S'MORES

Ingredients

Marshmallows
Graham Crackers
Bananas
Whipped Cream

Building Instructions

Frost half of a graham cracker with whipped cream. Slice bananas into pieces, and place the slices on top of the whipped cream. Toast marshmallow to the desired level. Place marshmallow on top of the banana slices. Sandwich the marshmallow and bananas together with another half of a graham cracker.

Chocolate-Covered
Espresso Bean S'mores

Ingredients

Marshmallows
Graham Crackers
Chocolate-Covered
    Espresso Beans

Building Instructions

Toast marshmallow to the
desired level. Place marshmallow on half
of a graham cracker. Poke chocolate-
covered espresso beans into the marshmallow.
Sandwich the marshmallow together with another half
of a graham cracker.

Apple Pie S'mores

Ingredients

Marshmallows
Cinnamon Graham Crackers
Apple Pie Filling

Building Instructions

Scoop 1 tablespoon of apple pie filling onto half of a
cinnamon graham cracker. Toast marshmallow to the
desired level. Place marshmallow on top of the apple
pie filling. Sandwich the marshmallow and pie filing
together with another half of a graham cracker.

Banana Split S'mores

Ingredients

- Marshmallows
- Graham Crackers
- Bananas
- Peanuts
- Chocolate Sundae Syrup

Building Instructions

Peel bananas and cut into slices. Place banana slices on half of a graham cracker. Drizzle chocolate sundae syrup over bananas. Sprinkle peanuts over the chocolate syrup. Toast marshmallow to the desired level. Place marshmallow on top of the bananas. Sandwich the marshmallow and bananas together with another half of a graham cracker.

Rice Krispie® Bar S'mores

Ingredients

Marshmallows
Rice Krispie Bars
Chocolate Bars

Prep Work

Combine Rice Krispie bar ingredients as directed on the side of the Rice Krispies box. Divide Rice Krispie bar mixture equally into two 9" x 13" pans. Flatten the mixture in each pan using a buttered fork. Bars should be $3/8$" thick. Allow bars to cool.

Building Instructions

Cut Rice Krispie bars into 2" x 2" squares. Place desired amount of chocolate on top of a Rice Krispie square. Toast marshmallow to the desired level. Place marshmallow on top of the chocolate. Sandwich the marshmallow and chocolate together with another Rice Krispie square.

NILLA® WAFER S'MORES

Ingredients

Marshmallows
Nilla Wafers
Cinnamon
Sugar

Prep Work

Combine 2 tablespoons of sugar with 1 teaspoon of cinnamon.

Building Instructions

Toast marshmallow to the desired level. Place marshmallow onto a Nilla wafer. Sprinkle cinnamon & sugar mixture over the toasted marshmallow. Sandwich the marshmallow with another Nilla wafer.

Nutter Butter® S'mores

Ingredients

Marshmallows
Nutter Butter Cookies

Building Instructions

Carefully pull apart a Nutter Butter cookie. Toast marshmallow to the desired level. Place marshmallow on half of the
Nutter Butter cookie. Sandwich the marshmallow together
with the remaining half of the Nutter Butter cookie.

Oatmeal Cream Pie S'mores

Ingredients

Marshmallows
Oatmeal Cookies
Vanilla Frosting

Building Instructions

Frost an oatmeal cookie with vanilla frosting. Toast marshmallow to the desired level. Place marshmallow on top of the vanilla frosting. Sandwich the marshmallow and frosting together with another oatmeal cookie.

More Graham Substitutes

These graham cracker replacements are so devilishly delicious that even the chocolate bar is optional!

1. Chocolate chip cookies
2. Ritz crackers
3. Chocolate shortbread cookies
4. Ginger cookies
5. Just about any cookie you can imagine!

Building Instructions

Toast marshmallow to the desired level. Place a marshmallow on top of a cookie or cracker. Sandwich the marshmallow together with another cookie or cracker.

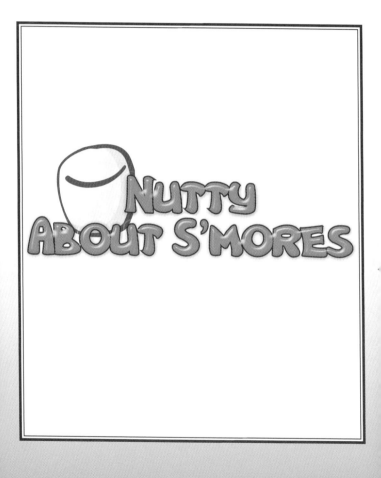

NUTTY ABOUT S'MORES

Pecan Fudge Cluster S'mores

Ingredients

Marshmallows
Graham Crackers
Chocolate Fudge Frosting
Pecans
Caramel Sundae Syrup

Building Instructions

Frost half of a graham cracker with fudge frosting. Cover fudge-frosted graham cracker with pecans. Drizzle caramel sundae syrup over pecans. Toast marshmallow to the desired level. Place marshmallow on top of the caramel-covered pecans. Sandwich the marshmallow and pecans together with another half of a graham cracker.

TRAIL MIX S'MORES

Ingredients

Marshmallows
Graham Crackers
Peanuts
M&Ms®
Raisins
Marshmallow Creme

Prep Work

To create trail mix, combine 1 cup
of peanuts with ½ cup of raisins and ½ cup of M&Ms.

Building Instructions

Frost half of a graham cracker with marshmallow creme.
Sprinkle trail mix onto the frosted graham cracker. Toast
marshmallow to the desired level. Place marshmallow on
top of the trail mix. Sandwich the marshmallow and trail mix
together with another half of a graham cracker.

White Chocolate Macadamia Nut S'mores

Ingredients

- Marshmallows
- Graham Crackers
- Caramel Sundae Syrup
- White Chocolate Bars
- Macadamia Nuts

Building Instructions

Place white chocolate pieces on half of a graham cracker. Drizzle caramel sundae syrup over the white chocolate. Place macadamia nuts on top of the caramel. Toast marshmallow to the desired level. Sandwich the marshmallow and macadamia nuts together with another half of a graham cracker.

Toasted Almond Fudge S'mores

Ingredients

Marshmallows
Graham Crackers
Chocolate Fudge Frosting
Almond Slices
Butter

Prep Work

In a microwave-safe pie plate, place ½ cup of almond slices and 1 tablespoon of butter. Microwave on high, stirring every minute until golden brown, approximately 4–5 minutes. This can also be done on a traditional stove.

Building Instructions

Frost half of a graham cracker with fudge frosting. Cover fudge-frosted graham cracker with almond slices. Toast marshmallow to the desired level. Place marshmallow on top of the fudge frosting and almond slices. Sandwich the marshmallow and almonds together with another half of a graham cracker.

Turtle S'mores

Ingredients

Marshmallows
Graham Crackers
Mr. Goodbar®
Caramel Sundae Syrup

Building Instructions

Place Mr. Goodbar pieces on half of a graham cracker. Drizzle caramel sundae syrup over the chocolate pieces. Toast marshmallow to the desired level. Sandwich the marshmallow and chocolate together with another half of a graham cracker.

Sweetheart S'mores

Ingredients

Marshmallows
Graham Crackers
Candy Conversation Hearts
Marshmallow Creme

Building Instructions

Frost half of a graham cracker with marshmallow creme. Place candy conversation hearts onto the frosted graham cracker. Toast marshmallow to the desired level. Place marshmallow on top of candy pieces. Sandwich the marshmallow and candy pieces together with another half of a graham cracker.

SPRING S'MORES

Ingredients

Peeps®
Graham Crackers
Chocolate Bars

Building Instructions

Place desired amount of chocolate on half of a graham
cracker. Carefully toast Peep to desired level. Since there is a
sugar coating on the outside of the Peep, it will burn faster.
Sandwich the Peep and chocolate together with another half
of a graham cracker.

Red, White & Blueberry S'mores

Ingredients

Marshmallows
Graham Crackers
Strawberry Jam
Fresh Blueberries

Building Instructions

Spread strawberry jam on half of a graham cracker. Place blueberries onto the jam-covered graham cracker. Toast marshmallow to the desired level. Place marshmallow on top of the blueberries. Sandwich the marshmallow and blueberries together with another half of a graham cracker.

Birthday Cake S'mores

Ingredients

Marshmallows
Graham Crackers
Leftover Birthday Cake
Frosting

Prep Work

Slice leftover birthday cake into approximately 2" x 1" pieces. The pieces of cake should be around half the size of a graham cracker.

Building Instructions

Place a piece of cake on half of a graham cracker. Use the frosting to cover all exposed sides of the cake. Toast marshmallow to the desired level. Place marshmallow on top of the frosted cake. Sandwich the marshmallow and cake together with another half of a graham cracker.

Note: For a birthday surprise, leave off the top graham cracker, and add a birthday candle.

Halloween S'mores

Ingredients

Marshmallows
Graham Crackers
Candy Corn

Building Instructions

On half of a graham cracker, place
candy corn. Toast marshmallow to
the desired level. Place marshmallow on
top of candy corn. Sandwich the marshmallow and
candy corn together with another half of a graham cracker.

Pumpkin Pie S'mores

Ingredients

Marshmallows
Graham Crackers
Canned Pumpkin Pie Filling
Whipped Cream

Building Instructions

Spread 1 tablespoon of pumpkin pie filling onto half of
a graham cracker. Toast marshmallow to the desired
level. Place marshmallow on top of the pumpkin pie filling.
Top with whipped cream. Sandwich the marshmallow, pie
filing and whipped cream together with another half of a
graham cracker.

CANDY CANE S'MORES

Ingredients

Marshmallows
Graham Crackers
Candy Canes
Chocolate Bars

Prep Work

In a large, resealable plastic bag, crush candy canes into fine pieces with a rolling pin.

Building Instructions

Place desired amount of chocolate on half of a graham cracker. Sprinkle candy cane pieces onto the chocolate. Toast marshmallow to the desired level. Place marshmallow on top of candy cane pieces. Sandwich the marshmallow and candy cane pieces together with another half of a graham cracker.

Kahlua® Brownie S'mores

Ingredients

Marshmallows
Graham Crackers
Brownies
Kahlua Liquor

Prep Work

Using your favorite brownie mix, prepare as directed on the package. Use the largest pan size to make thin brownies. Bake and cool. With a fork, poke holes into the brownies at 1-inch intervals. Using a pastry brush, apply a coating of Kahlua to the top of the brownies. Let the first coating of Kahlua saturate into the brownies. Apply a second coating of Kahlua. Cut brownies into 2" x 2" squares.

Building Instructions

Toast marshmallow to the desired level. Place a brownie and the toasted marshmallow on half of a graham cracker. Sandwich marshmallow and the brownie together with another half of a graham cracker.

Grasshopper S'mores

Ingredients

Marshmallows
Graham Crackers
Chocolate Bars
Vanilla Frosting
Crème de Menthe
Crème de Cocoa

Prep Work

To 1 cup of vanilla frosting, add ½ shot of crème de menthe and ½ shot of crème de cocoa. Mix until smooth. Chill.

Building Instructions

Frost half of a graham cracker with frosting mixture. Place chocolate bar pieces onto the frosted graham cracker. Toast marshmallow to the desired level. Place marshmallow on top of chocolate pieces. Sandwich the marshmallow and chocolate bar pieces together with another half of a graham cracker.

Irish Cream S'mores

Ingredients

Marshmallows
Graham Crackers
Chocolate Bars
Vanilla Frosting
Irish Cream Liquor

Prep Work

To 1 cup of vanilla frosting, add
one shot of Irish Cream. Mix until
smooth. Chill.

Building Instructions

Frost half of a graham cracker with frosting mixture. Place
chocolate bar pieces onto the frosted graham cracker. Toast
marshmallow to the desired level. Place marshmallow on top
of chocolate pieces. Sandwich the marshmallow and chocolate
bar pieces together with another half of a graham cracker.

Jell-O® Shot S'mores

Ingredients

Marshmallows
Graham Crackers
Jell-O® Gelatin (any flavor)
Whipped Cream
Vodka

Prep Work

Combine 1 cup of boiling water with 1 small box of gelatin.
After the gelatin powder has dissolved, add ½ cup of vodka.
Mix and pour into a 9" x 13" pan. Chill until gelatin sets. Cut
gelatin into 2" x 2" squares.

Building Instructions

Spread whipped cream on half of a graham cracker. Place a
gelatin square on top of the whipped cream. Toast marshmallow to the desired level. Place marshmallow on top of
the gelatin square. Sandwich the marshmallow and gelatin
together with another half of a graham cracker.

Note: Most types of clear alcohol can be substituted for the
vodka. Rum is also a very tasty alternative.

Strawberry Cream Cheese
S'mores & Champagne

Ingredients

Marshmallows
Graham Crackers
Strawberries
Cream Cheese
Champagne

Building Instructions

Clean strawberries and remove stems. Cut strawberries
into slices. Spread cream cheese on half of a graham cracker.
Place strawberry slices onto the cream-cheese-covered
graham cracker. Toast marshmallow to the desired level.
Place marshmallow on top of the strawberries. Sandwich
the marshmallow and strawberries together with another
half of a graham cracker. Serve with a side of champagne.

Rum Cake S'mores

Ingredients

Marshmallows
Graham Crackers
Vanilla Cake
Rum

Prep Work

Using your favorite vanilla cake mix,
prepare as directed on package. Pour
mix into a 9" x 13" pan. Bake and let cool.
With the handle of a wooden spoon, poke holes into the
cake at 1-inch intervals. Fill the holes to the top with rum,
and chill the cake for at least 1 hour. The cake will absorb the
rum and become very moist. Cut the cake into 2" x 1" pieces,
about the size of half of a graham cracker.

Building Instructions

Toast marshmallow to the desired level. Place a piece of cake
and the toasted marshmallow on half of a graham cracker.
Sandwich the marshmallow and cake together
with another half of a graham cracker.

Lemon Cheesecake S'mores

Ingredients

Marshmallows
Graham Crackers
Cream Cheese
Limoncello

Prep Work

Soften 8 ounces of cream cheese in a mixing bowl. Add
1 shot of limoncello and mix thoroughly. Chill.

Building Instructions

Spread cream cheese on half of a graham cracker. Toast
marshmallow to the desired level. Place marshmallow on top
of the cream cheese. Sandwich the marshmallow and cream
cheese together with another half of a graham cracker.

Alternative Heat Sources

S'mores are traditionally made around the campfire. However, here are some additional heat sources that you can use for marshmallow toasting. Regardless of the heat source, the method of toasting remains the same as those found on pages 10–11.

- Grill
- Microwave
- Stove (Kitchen or Camp)
- S'mores Maker

Some people also use candles, but I don't endorse this. Especially indoors, it can be a fire hazard—and besides, the candle wax and other possible residues give the marshmallow a funny taste!

Did You Know?

Mark your calendar! August 10 of every year is (unofficially) recognized as National S'more Day. Do you need a better reason for a campfire?

S'more Do's and Don'ts

- Do get your s'more top and bottom set up before roasting your marshmallows. This allows you to enjoy your s'more while the marshmallow is still warm.

- Do store leftover marshmallows in an airtight zipper bag to help keep them fresh.

- Do keep a very close eye on marshmallows heated in the microwave. It only takes a few seconds for them to heat up —and only a few more for them to explode!

- Don't skimp on the ingredients. You'll get a tastier s'more with more generous portions.

- Don't leave your s'more unattended. Someone is likely to steal it.

S'more Safety Tips

- Always make sure an adult is present when heating marsh-mallows at home and out in the wild. For that matter, leave campfire preparation to the grown-ups too.

- When purchasing roasting forks, choose longer forks that will allow you to stand farther away from the fire.

- If your marshmallow catches fire, never wave your fork in the air to put out the flames. Instead blow them out.

- Always give your marshmallow some time to cool off before handling or biting into it.

- Never let your campfire burn unattended. Extinguish it completely before leaving.

- If you lose a marshmallow in the campfire . . . just let it go!

Clean-up Tips

- Soak used utensils in hot, soapy water immediately after use.

- Scrub roasting forks with steel wool soap pads.

- Spray utensils with non-stick spray before using them. Do not spray near open flame!

- Always clean your area and pick up all garbage. Leave the outdoors better than you found it.

Did You Know?

Marshmallows are named as such because they were originally made with sap from the root of a marsh mallow plant. Nowadays they're mostly just a mixture of water, gelatin and sugar.

My Recipe:

Ingredients

Prep Work

Building Instructions

My Recipe:

Ingredients

Prep Work

Building Instructions

My Recipe:

Ingredients

Prep Work

Building Instructions

My Recipe:

Ingredients

Prep Work

Building Instructions

My Recipe:

Ingredients

Prep Work

Building Instructions

My Recipe:

Ingredients

Prep Work

Building Instructions

About the Author

Becky Rasmussen was born and raised in rural Minnesota
and is a graduate of the University of Wisconsin-Eau Claire.
She has spent most of her life involved in outdoor activities,
such as hunting, fishing, boating, camping and traveling. She
enjoys cooking for her friends and family, both in the kitchen
and around the campfire. As a camp counselor and seasonal
park employee she has spent many years helping adults and
children learn to enjoy and explore the outdoors.